THE BEST OF
POETRY IN MOTION

CELEBRATING TWENTY-FIVE YEAR.

W. W. NORTON & COMPANY

Independent Publishers Since 1923

NEW YORK | LONDON

THE BEST OF
POETRY IN
MOTION

N SUBWAYS AND BUSES

EDITED BY ALICE QUINN

FOREWORD BY BILLY COLLINS

For information about permission to reproduce selections from this book,
write to Permissions, W. W. Norton & Company, Inc.,
500 Fifth Avenue, New York, NY 10110

For information about special discounts for bulk purchases, please contact
W. W. Norton Special Sales at specialsales@wwnorton.com or 800-233-4830

Manufacturing by Toppan Leefung
Book design by JAM Design
Production manager: Anna Oler

ISBN 978-0-393-60937-0

W. W. Norton & Company, Inc.
500 Fifth Avenue, New York, N.Y. 10110
www.wwnorton.com

W. W. Norton & Company Ltd.
15 Carlisle Street, London W1D 3BS

1 2 3 4 5 6 7 8 9 0

To the poets, the riders, the readers!

Contents

Preface

This book celebrates twenty-five years of an enduringly popular program, reaching eight and a half million riders on public transit in New York City every day.

Elise Paschen, one of the founders of the program when she was executive director of the Poetry Society of America, has described how it was modeled after one in London much as the Poetry Society of America followed suit a year after the Poetry Society of England was established in 1909. In her own telling, on a Poetry Society reading tour of England with Native American women poets, she "spotted a sonnet by Michael Drayton on the London Tube and fantasized about featuring poems on subway cars and buses in New York City." Legend has it that around the same time, Alan Kiepper, then president of MTA New York City Transit, also visiting England, was similarly inspired by the notion of poems on public transportation and upon his return contacted the PSA to join forces and bring the program into being.

Poetry in Motion flourished with support from New York City Transit, which continues today. In the words of MTA New York City Transit interim Executive Director Veronique Hakim, "I must confess that *Poetry in Motion* is my main exposure to poetry these days, and I cherish its impact on me and the countless commuters who clearly love it."

In 2012, Sandra Bloodworth, director of MTA Arts & Design, seized an opportunity to bring new direction and vitality to the program by pairing the poems with the amazing trove of imagery from Arts & Design's artwork commissioned since 1985. Twenty-two poems that reflect this collaborative approach and exciting new design appear here.

One of the first of the poems to appear in the new format is by Jeffrey Yang, posted in the system in 2012. In an exuberant letter, he wrote of the experience, "I cannot begin to describe the response I've received and continue to receive from friends and strangers who have found the poem unexpectedly around the city. One film director has used it in his new movie, a musician has set it to music, many friends have described spur-of-the-moment discussions with other train riders about it, a philosopher started a long blog thread discussion on it, a literary critic used it as an epigraph in her new book, a nun wrote me a glowing note about it, random people post stills of it on the internet, and just last week a letterpress printer contacted me out of the blue about seeing it—the list goes on and on and is just astonishing."

Responding to a publisher's questionnaire tucked in a

new collection of poems by Chase Twichell, whose poem was posted in 2013, reader Amelia Bell wrote, "I saw this poem—'To the Reader: Twilight'—on a NYC subway where there are usually ads, and now it is cold but sunny outside, and I am imagining a world where poetry circles us in the public spaces like wild birds, and it's wonderful."

For millions, the program is embedded in daily life. Liriel Higa, a former assistant to *New York Times* columnist Nicholas Kristof, snapped a picture of him in a subway car flanked by Patrick Phillips' poem "Heaven" and quipped in a piece for the newspaper's blog, "He also is capable of writing his column anywhere, whether a subway car or a jostling car on an unpaved road. Heaven, for him, is fast Wi-Fi and getting people to care about a neglected issue."

The program that launched in 1992 with four poems by Emily Dickinson, Walt Whitman, Lucille Clifton, and W. B. Yeats has since then held aloft hundreds of poems, and millions of appreciative New Yorkers have never known a time when there *weren't* poems on public transit. To quote Jeffrey Yang once more, "To get it off the ground those many years ago took risk and vision, while to keep it going has taken perseverance and dedication."

We have chosen one hundred poems from this resplendent bounty of work, poems necessarily short in order to be visually legible at a distance, plus a few excerpts that we couldn't resist presenting in the program and reprinting here. As Molly Peacock, former president of the PSA and another founder of *Poetry in Motion*, has written, "Since nationalities representing the entire world ride on New York City's public transit, we try to reflect that world. We look for poems that will speak to all ethnicities, genders, ages. We look for voices that will stimulate the exhausted, inspire the frustrated, comfort the burdened, and enchant even the youngest passengers."

We know that you will enjoy reading, rereading, sharing, and perhaps even memorizing the selections from this beloved program in its first twenty-five years.

ALICE QUINN
Executive Director
Poetry Society of America

Foreword: The Turning Wheels of Poetry

Billy Collins

t's a rainy Tuesday morning in February and you're riding to work on a downtown 6 train. I should add that you do not like your job. Your boss—that's how he thinks of himself—has a habit of poking his head into your cubicle to look over your shoulder at your screen. In the afternoon, he reeks of pastrami. Anyway, your daily journey to work has begun. All the seats are taken, so you stand, sharing a pole with five other hands, and you follow the first rule of New York City subway comportment: Do not make eye contact. With anyone. You look at the floor. You study a button on the coat of the person next to you. You look up at the row of gaudy ads offering free legal advice, cheap flights to the Caribbean, and a cure for acne guaranteed by one Dr. Zitsmore, or at least that's what his name sounds like. Then, just as you are giving small thanks for not being in one of those cars that are plastered with one huge thematic ad for a single product—typically vodka and it's too early to think about vodka—you notice a little cluster of words.

> Don't worry, spiders,
> I keep house
>   casually.

Is your outlook not brightened? Is your heart not enlarged if only slightly? Has this little poem (a haiku by the Japanese poet Issa) not refreshed you, even made you feel less claustrophobic in the crowded car? The poem is clearly different from everything else on the train. The advertisements, of course, are selling all kinds of things, but the poem is not selling anything except itself, declaring its own existence right there before your eyes. The poem is not a pitch, but an offering, a gift. If its singular presence, not in a book with other poems but on a subway car, seems incongruous, it's because it stands apart from the business of "getting and spending." The poem is free—in more ways than one.

The *Poetry in Motion* program, which plants poems in unlikely places, is sponsored by the Poetry Society of America, based in Manhattan, and the Metropolitan Transit Authority of New York, but the program is also a part of a wider national effort developed vigorously over the past twenty years to situate poems in the paths of people as they travel from one place to another. By liberating poems from the libraries and classrooms where they are traditionally housed and studied, groups like the PSA and the MTA hope to make poetry a part of everyday life, something more than a unit in a school's curriculum.

A poem that you notice on a bus comes at you too fast for you to resist. You might even read it before you realize it's a poem. It's one thing to commit an intentional act of literary appreciation by repairing to your study and opening a beloved volume of John Keats or Elizabeth Barrett Browning, and quite another thing to be taken unawares by a short poem that you spot as you are riding on a subway, or driving past a billboard, or looking up to notice a small plane dragging a line of poetry high above the length of a beach on a summer's day. Such unexpected encounters with poetry can provide a sudden sense of mental and even spiritual nourishment by connecting us with the deeply human realms of love and loss, joy and death, as well as reminding us that beyond the routine of our daily travel there lies the wider world of clouds and onions, plums and antelopes, rivers and hedgehogs—the great sensorium of human experience.

Poetry on the fly is essential to this program, but its popularity has led to the present printed volume, a selection of some of the many *Poetry in Motion* poems that have appeared on various forms of public transportation, delivering solace and insight to millions of riders. Here, poems once in motion have come to rest in a book, but they continue to move their readers. And what an imaginative variety of poetic delights is on offer. Kenneth Koch introduces us to a talking cloud. The sight of mangoes and bananas brings Claude McKay to tears. Robert Frost mixes fireflies and stars. Emily Dickinson tells us "How happy is the little stone / That rambles in the road alone." Marilyn Chin sweeps autumn leaves. Fanny Howe leads us into a nonexistent city with real poppies and finches. Hopkins gives us varied reasons to "Praise him." Ferlinghetti invokes "the little airplanes of the heart." Sharon Olds speaks of marriage and Moo Shu Pork. Tess Gallagher must stop writing to fold the clothes. And all Nina Cassian wants is for some younger passenger to offer her a seat.

Yes, there is much to savor in this gathering, but before you dig in, let us return for a moment to the downtown 6 train. Only now it's a pleasant morning, a Thursday in April. Much better weather, cool and sunny. You're on your way to work again. The boss still smells like pastrami, but today you've found a seat. You slide in between two strangers who scooch over to make room. You sigh for no reason. Or is it the familiarity of the scene that brings about your melancholy? At every stop, people get off and new people get on, which might be why you start thinking of someone you miss as the train hurtles underground. And that's when you glance up and read:

Separation

Your absence has gone through me
Like thread through a needle.
Everything I do is stitched with its color.

W. S. MERWIN

You just experienced a connection you may never forget, and your workday is off to a flier.

THE BEST OF
POETRY IN
MOTION

Along the hard crest of the snowdrift

Along the hard crest of the snowdrift
to my white, mysterious house,
both of us quiet now,
keeping silent as we walk.
And sweeter than any song
this dream we now complete—
the trembling of branches we brush against,
the soft ringing of your spurs.

ANNA AKHMATOVA
(1889–1966)
Translated, from the Russian, by Jane Kenyon

from **My Grandmother's New York Apartment**

Everything pulled out or folded away:
sofa into a bed, tray tables that dis-
appear behind a door, everything
transmutable, alchemy in small
spaces, even my grandmother tiny
and changeable: a housecoat and rollers
which vanish and become an Irish
tweed suit, a tilted chapeau, a Hello
in the elevator just like, as she
would say, the Queen of Denmark.

ELIZABETH ALEXANDER
(b. 1962)

Awaking in New York

Curtains forcing their will
against the wind,
children sleep,
exchanging dreams with
seraphim. The city
drags itself awake on
subway straps; and
I, an alarm, awake as a
rumor of war,
lie stretching into dawn,
unasked and unheeded.

MAYA ANGELOU
(1928–2014)

Awaking in New York

Maya Angelou (1928-2014)

Curtains forcing their will
against the wind,
children sleep,
exchanging dreams with
seraphim. The city
drags itself awake on
subway straps; and
I, an alarm, awake as a
rumor of war,
lie stretching into dawn,
unasked and unheeded.

William Low, *A Day in Parkchester*, 2011

from O Tell Me the Truth About Love

When it comes, will it come without warning
   Just as I'm picking my nose?
Will it knock on my door in the morning,
   Or tread in the bus on my toes?
Will it come like a change in the weather?
   Will its greeting be courteous or rough?
Will it alter my life altogether?
   O tell me the truth about love.

W. H. AUDEN
(1907–1973)

Stay

Now the journey is ending,
the wind is losing heart.
Into your hands it's falling,
a rickety house of cards.

The cards are backed with pictures
displaying all the world.
You've stacked up all the images
and shuffled them with words.

And how profound the playing
that once again begins!
Stay, the card you're drawing
is the only world you'll win.

INGEBORG BACHMANN
(1926–1973)
Translated, from the German, by Peter Filkins

Conversation (*from* Four Poems)

The tumult in the heart
keeps asking questions.
And then it stops and undertakes to answer
in the same tone of voice.
No one could tell the difference.

Uninnocent, these conversations start,
and then engage the senses,
only half-meaning to.
And then there is no choice,
and then there is no sense;

until a name
and all its connotation are the same.

ELIZABETH BISHOP
(1911–1979)

from **The Tyger**

When the stars threw down their spears
And water'd heaven with their tears:
Did he smile his work to see?
Did he who made the Lamb make thee?

Tyger Tyger burning bright,
In the forests of the night:
What immortal hand or eye,
Dare frame thy fearful symmetry?

WILLIAM BLAKE
(1757–1827)

To My Dear and Loving Husband

If ever two were one, then surely we.
If ever man were loved by wife, then thee;
If ever wife was happy in a man,
Compare with me, ye women, if you can.
I prize thy love more than whole mines of gold,
Or all the riches that the East doth hold.
My love is such that rivers cannot quench,
Nor ought but love from thee give recompense.
Thy love is such I can no way repay;
The heavens reward thee manifold, I pray.
Then while we live, in love let's so persever,
That when we live no more, we may live ever.

ANNE BRADSTREET
(1612–1672)

Speech to the Young: Speech to the Progress-Toward (Among them Nora and Henry III)

Say to them,
say to the down-keepers,
the sun-slappers,
the self-soilers,
the harmony-hushers,
"Even if you are not ready for day
it cannot always be night."
You will be right.
For that is the hard home-run.

Live not for battles won.
Live not for the-end-of-the-song.
Live in the along.

GWENDOLYN BROOKS
(1917–2000)

Please Give This Seat to an Elderly or Disabled Person

I stood during the entire journey:
nobody offered me a seat
although I was at least a hundred years older than anyone
    else on board,
although the signs of at least three major afflictions
were visible on me:
Pride, Loneliness, and Art.

NINA CASSIAN
(1924–2014)
Translated, from the Romanian, by Naomi Lazard

El Chicle
(for Marcel)

Mi'jo and I were laughing—*ha, ha, ha*—
when the gum he chewed fell out of his mouth
and into my hair which, after I clipped it,
flew in the air, on the back of a dragonfly
that dipped in the creek and was snapped fast
by a turtle that reached high and swam deep.
Mi'jo wondered what happened to that gum,
worried that it stuck to the back
of my seat and Mami will be mad when
she can't get it out. Meanwhile,
the turtle in the pond that ate the dragonfly
that carried the hair
with the gum on its back
swam South and hasn't been seen once
since.

ANA CASTILLO
(b. 1953)

Autumn Leaves

The dead piled up, thick, fragrant, on the fire escape.
My mother ordered me again, and again, to sweep it clean.
All that blooms must fall. I learned this not from the Dao,
    but from high school biology.

Oh, the contradictions of having a broom and not a dustpan!
I swept the leaves down, down through the iron grille
and let the dead rain over the Wong family's patio.

And it was Achilles Wong who completed the task.
    We called her:
The-one-who-cleared-away-another-family's-autumn.
She blossomed, tall, benevolent, notwithstanding.

MARILYN CHIN
(b. 1955)

Hedgehog

He ambles along like a walking pin cushion,
Stops and curls up like a chestnut burr.
He's not worried because he's so little.
Nobody is going to slap him around.

CHU CHEN PO
(9th century)
Translated, from the Chinese, by Kenneth Rexroth

You Called Me *Corazón*

That was enough
for me to forgive you.
To spirit a tiger
from its cell.

Called me *corazón*
in that instant before
I let go the phone
back to its cradle.

Your voice small.
Heat of your eyes,
how I would've placed
my mouth on each.

Said *corazón*
and the word blazed
like a branch of *jacaranda*.

SANDRA CISNEROS
(b. 1954)

let there be new flowering

let there be new flowering
in the fields let the fields
turn mellow for the men
let the men keep tender
through the time let the time
be wrested from the war
let the war be won
let love be
at the end

LUCILLE CLIFTON
(1936–2010)

Subway

As you fly swiftly underground
with a song in your ears
or lost in the maze of a book,

remember the ones who descended here
into the mire of bedrock
to bore a hole through this granite,

to clear a passage for you
where there was only darkness and stone.
Remember as you come up into the light.

BILLY COLLINS
(b. 1941)

Subway Billy Collins, b. 1941

As you fly swiftly underground
with a song in your ears
or lost in the maze of a book,

remember the ones who descended here
into the mire of bedrock
to bore a hole through this granite,

to clear a passage for you
where there was only darkness and stone.
Remember as you come up into the light.

Sarah Sze, *Blueprint for a Landscape*, 2016

Love opened a mortal wound

Love opened a mortal wound.
In agony, I worked the blade
to make it deeper. Please,
I begged, let death come quick.

Wild, distracted, sick,
I counted, counted
all the ways love hurt me.
One life, I thought—a thousand deaths.

Blow after blow, my heart
couldn't survive this beating.
Then—how can I explain it?

I came to my senses. I said,
Why do I suffer? What lover
ever had so much pleasure?

SOR JUANA INÉS DE LA CRUZ
(1651–1695)
Translated, from the Spanish, by Joan Larkin and
Jaime Manrique

How happy is the little stone
That rambles in the road alone,
And doesn't care about careers,
And exigencies never fears;
Whose coat of elemental brown
A passing universe put on;
And independent as the sun,
Associates or glows alone,
Fulfilling absolute decree
In casual simplicity.

EMILY DICKINSON
(1830–1886)

Adolescence—I

In water-heavy nights behind grandmother's porch
We knelt in the tickling grasses and whispered:
Linda's face hung before us, pale as a pecan,
And it grew wise as she said:
      "A boy's lips are soft,
       As soft as baby's skin."
The air closed over her words.
A firefly whirred near my ear, and in the distance
I could hear streetlamps ping
Into miniature suns
Against a feathery sky.

RITA DOVE
(b. 1952)

from **Sympathy**

I know why the caged bird sings, ah me,
    When his wing is bruised and his bosom sore,—
When he beats his bars and he would be free;
It is not a carol of joy or glee,
    But a prayer that he sends from his heart's deep core,
But a plea, that upward to Heaven he flings—
I know why the caged bird sings!

PAUL LAURENCE DUNBAR
(1872–1906)

from **The Love Song of J. Alfred Prufrock**

Let us go then, you and I,
When the evening is spread out against the sky
Like a patient etherized upon a table;
Let us go, through certain half-deserted streets,
The muttering retreats
Of restless nights in one-night cheap hotels
And sawdust restaurants with oyster-shells:
Streets that follow like a tedious argument
Of insidious intent
To lead you to an overwhelming question . . .
Oh, do not ask, "What is it?"
Let us go and make our visit.

T. S. ELIOT
(1888–1965)

Birth

When they were wild
When they were not yet human
When they could have been anything,
I was on the other side ready with milk to lure them,
And their father, too, each name a net in his hands.

LOUISE ERDRICH
(b. 1954)

The Ideal

This is where I came from.
I passed this way.
This should not be shameful
Or hard to say.

A self is a self.
It is not a screen.
A person should respect
What he has been.

This is my past
Which I shall not discard.
This is the ideal.
This is hard.

JAMES FENTON
(b. 1949)

Sandinista Avioncitos

The little airplanes of the heart
with their brave little propellers
What can they do
against the winds of darkness
even as butterflies are beaten back
by hurricanes
yet do not die
They lie in wait wherever
they can hide and hang
their fine wings folded
and when the killer-wind dies
they flutter forth again
into the new-blown light
live as leaves

LAWRENCE FERLINGHETTI
(b. 1919)

Fireflies in the Garden

Here come real stars to fill the upper skies,
And here on earth come emulating flies,
That though they never equal stars in size,
(And they were never really stars at heart)
Achieve at times a very star-like start.
Only, of course, they can't sustain the part.

ROBERT FROST
(1874–1963)

I Stop Writing the Poem

to fold the clothes. No matter who lives
or who dies, I'm still a woman.
I'll always have plenty to do.
I bring the arms of his shirt
together. Nothing can stop
our tenderness. I'll get back
to the poem. I'll get back to being
a woman. But for now
there's a shirt, a giant shirt
in my hands, and somewhere a small girl
standing next to her mother
watching to see how it's done.

TESS GALLAGHER
(b. 1943)

VARIACION / VARIATIONS

El remanso del aire
bajo la rama del eco.

El remanso del agua
bajo fronda de luceros.

El remanso de tu boca
bajo espesura de besos.

.

The still waters of the air
under the bough of the echo.

The still waters of the water
under a frond of stars.

The still waters of your mouth
under a thicket of kisses.

FEDERICO GARCÍA LORCA
(1898–1936)
Translated, from the Spanish, by Lysander Kemp

Winter Poem

once a snowflake fell
on my brow and i loved
it so much and i kissed
it and it was happy and called its cousins
and brothers and a web
of snow engulfed me then
i reached to love them all
and i squeezed them and they became
a spring rain and i stood perfectly
still and was a flower

NIKKI GIOVANNI
(b. 1943)

Noche de Lluvia, San Salvador

Rain who nails the earth,
whose infinite legs
nail the earth, whose silver faces
touch my faces, I marry you. & open
all the windows of my house to hear
your million feral versions
of si si

           sí

     si

            si

ARACELIS GIRMAY
(b. 1977)

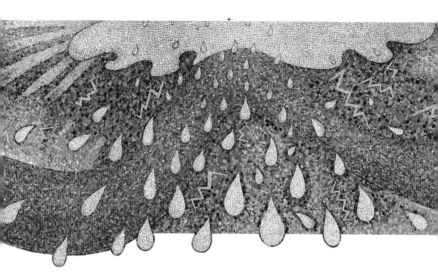

Noche de Lluvia, San Salvador
Aracelis Girmay, b. 1977

Rain who nails the earth,
whose infinite legs
nail the earth, whose silver faces
touch my faces, I marry you. & open
all the windows of my house to hear
your million feral versions
of si si
               sí

          si

                 si

Poetry in Motion

First Memory

Long ago, I was wounded. I lived
to revenge myself
against my father, not
for what he was—
for what I was: from the beginning of time,
in childhood, I thought
that pain meant
I was not loved.
It meant I loved.

LOUISE GLÜCK
(b. 1943)

Lady Liberty

All stars lead to this city,
she's an angel unfolding midnight
a river of invisible trumpets
and sidewalks of moons,
she's the blues
drunk on the light
commuting with love
on a sailboat
that's found
the perfect island.

NATHALIE HANDAL
(b. 1969)

Lady Liberty

Nathalie Handal b.1969

All stars lead to this city,
she's an angel unfolding midnight
a river of invisible trumpets
and sidewalks of moons,
she's the blues
drunk on the light
commuting with love
on a sailboat
that's found
the perfect island.

Olimpia Zagnoli, *New York View*, 2014

from **Emergence**

A human mind is small when thinking
of small things.
It is large when embracing the maker
of walking, thinking and flying.
If I can locate the sense beyond desire,
I will not eat or drink
until I stagger into the earth
with grief.
I will locate the point of dawning
and awaken
with the longest day in the world.

JOY HARJO
(b. 1951)

Those Winter Sundays

Sundays too my father got up early
and put his clothes on in the blueblack cold,
then with cracked hands that ached
from labor in the weekday weather made
banked fires blaze. No one ever thanked him.

I'd wake and hear the cold splintering, breaking.
When the rooms were warm, he'd call,
and slowly I would rise and dress,
fearing the chronic angers of that house,

Speaking indifferently to him,
who had driven out the cold
and polished my good shoes as well.
What did I know, what did I know
of love's austere and lonely offices?

ROBERT HAYDEN
(1913–1980)

Scaffolding Seamus Heaney, 1939-2013

Masons, when they start upon a building,
Are careful to test out the scaffolding;

Make sure that planks won't slip at busy points,
Secure all ladders, tighten bolted joints.

And yet all this comes down when the job's done
Showing off walls of sure and solid stone.

So if, my dear, there sometimes seem to be
Old bridges breaking between you and me

Never fear. We may let the scaffolds fall
Confident that we have built our wall.

Poetry in Motion

Jean Shin, *Elevated*

Scaffolding

Masons, when they start upon a building,
Are careful to test out the scaffolding;

Make sure that planks won't slip at busy points,
Secure all ladders, tighten bolted joints.

And yet all this comes down when the job's done
Showing off walls of sure and solid stone.

So if, my dear, there sometimes seem to be
Old bridges breaking between you and me

Never fear. We may let the scaffolds fall
Confident that we have built our wall.

SEAMUS HEANEY
(1939–2013)

I Am Singing the Cold Rain

for charles white antelope

ni hoi nim mi ni hon   ido mi moo
ni hoi nim mi ni hon   e inif
ni hoi das i woi nu
na wodstan ni hi vist
na dutz   na ho utz

.

i am singing the cold rain
i am singing the winter dawn
i am turning in the gray morning
of my life
toward home

LANCE HENSON
(b. 1944)
Translated from the Cheyenne

Pied Beauty

Glory be to God for dappled things—
    For skies of couple-colour as a brinded cow;
      For rose-moles all in stipple upon trout that swim;
Fresh-firecoal chestnut-falls; finches' wings;
    Landscape plotted and pieced—fold, fallow, and plough;
      And all trades, their gear and tackle and trim.

All things counter, original, spare, strange;
    Whatever is fickle, freckled (who knows how?)
      With swift, slow; sweet, sour; adazzle, dim;
He fathers-forth whose beauty is past change:
                        Praise him.

GERARD MANLEY HOPKINS
(1844–1889)

You travel a path on paper
and discover you're in a city
you only thought about before.

It's a Sunday marketplace. Parakeets and finches
are placed on the stones
and poppies in transparent wrapping.

How can you be where you never were?
And how did you find the way—with your mind
your only measure?

FANNY HOWE
(b. 1940)

Luck

Sometimes a crumb falls
From the tables of joy,
Sometimes a bone
Is flung.

To some people
Love is given,
To others
Only heaven.

LANGSTON HUGHES
(1902–1967)

Parlour-Piece

With love so like fire they dared not
Let it out into strawy small talk;
With love so like a flood they dared not
Let out a trickle lest the whole crack,

These two sat speechlessly:
Pale cool tea in tea-cups chaperoned
Stillness, silence, the eyes
Where fire and flood strained.

TED HUGHES
(1930–1998)

Two Haiku

Don't worry, spiders,
I keep house
    casually.

Mosquito at my ear—
does it think
    I'm deaf?

KOBAYASHI ISSA
(1763–1828)
Translated, from the Japanese, by Robert Hass

Leave It All Up to Me

All we want is to succumb to a single kiss
that will contain us like a marathon
with no finish line, and if so, that we land
like newspapers before sunrise, halcyon
mornings like blue martinis. I am learning
the steps to a foreign song: her mind
was torpedo, and her body was storm,
a kind of *Wow*. All we want is a metropolis
of Sundays, an empire of hand-holding
and park benches. She says, "Leave it all up to me."

MAJOR JACKSON
(b. 1968)

Louis Delsarte, *Transitions*, 2001

Leave It All Up to Me   Major Jackson, b. 1968

All we want is to succumb to a single kiss
that will contain us like a marathon
with no finish line, and if so, that we land
like newspapers before sunrise, halcyon
mornings like blue martinis. I am learning
the steps to a foreign song: her mind
was torpedo, and her body was storm,
a kind of *Wow*. All we want is a metropolis
of Sundays, an empire of hand-holding
and park benches. She says, "Leave it all up to me."

from **To Autumn**

Season of mists and mellow fruitfulness,
  Close bosom-friend of the maturing sun;
Conspiring with him how to load and bless
  With fruit the vines that round the thatch-eaves run;
To bend with apples the moss'd cottage-trees,
  And fill all fruit with ripeness to the core;
    To swell the gourd, and plump the hazel shells
  With a sweet kernel; to set budding more,
  And still more, later flowers for the bees,
  Until they think warm days will never cease,
    For summer has o'er-brimm'd their clammy cells.

JOHN KEATS
(1795–1821)

The Suitor

We lie back to back. Curtains
lift and fall,
like the chest of someone sleeping.
Wind moves the leaves of the box elder;
they show their light undersides,
turning all at once
like a school of fish.
Suddenly I understand that I am happy.
For months this feeling
has been coming closer, stopping
for short visits, like a timid suitor.

JANE KENYON
(1947–1995)

Hide-and-Seek 1933

Galway Kinnell, (1927 - 2014)

Once when we were playing
hide-and-seek and it was time
to go home, the rest gave up
on the game before it was done
and forgot I was still hiding.
I remained hidden as a matter
of honor until the moon rose.

William Low, *A Day in Parkchester*, 2011

Hide-and-Seek 1933

Once when we were playing
hide-and-seek and it was time
to go home, the rest gave up
on the game before it was done
and forgot I was still hiding.
I remained hidden as a matter
of honor until the moon rose.

GALWAY KINNELL
(1927–2014)

A Big Clown-Face-Shaped Cloud

You just went by
With no one to see you, practically.
You were in good shape, for a cloud,
With perhaps several minutes more to exist.
You were speaking, or seemed to be,
Mouth open wide, talking, to a
Belted angel-shaped cloud that was riding ahead.

KENNETH KOCH
(1925–2002)

A Map of the World

One of the ancient maps of the world
is heart-shaped, carefully drawn
and once washed with bright colors,
though the colors have faded
as you might expect feelings to fade
from a fragile old heart, the brown map
of a life. But feeling is indelible,
and longing infinite, a starburst compass
pointing in all the directions
two lovers might go, a fresh breeze
swelling their sails, the future uncharted,
still far from the edge
where the sea pours into the stars.

TED KOOSER
(b. 1939)

A Map of the World Ted Kooser b. 1939

One of the ancient maps of the world
is heart-shaped, carefully drawn
and once washed with bright colors,
though the colors have faded
as you might expect feelings to fade
from a fragile old heart, the brown map
of a life. But feeling is indelible,
and longing infinite, a starburst compass
pointing in all the directions
two lovers might go, a fresh breeze
swelling their sails, the future uncharted,
still far from the edge
where the sea pours into the stars.

An Old Cracked Tune

My name is Solomon Levi,
the desert is my home,
my mother's breast was thorny,
and father I had none.

The sands whispered, *Be separate,*
the stones taught me, *Be hard.*
I dance, for the joy of surviving,
on the edge of the road.

STANLEY KUNITZ
(1905–2006)

I Ask My Mother to Sing

She begins, and my grandmother joins her.
Mother and daughter sing like young girls.
If my father were alive, he would play
his accordion and sway like a boat.

I've never been in Peking, or the Summer Palace,
nor stood on the great Stone Boat to watch
the rain begin on Kuen Ming Lake, the picnickers
running away in the grass.

But I love to hear it sung;
how the waterlilies fill with rain until
they overturn, spilling water into water,
then rock back, and fill with more.

Both women have begun to cry,
but neither stops her song.

LI-YOUNG LEE
(b. 1957)

Suspended

I had grasped God's garment in the void
but my hand slipped
on the rich silk of it.
The 'everlasting arms' my sister loved to remember
must have upheld my leaden weight
from falling, even so,
for though I claw at empty air and feel
nothing, no embrace,
I have not plummeted.

DENISE LEVERTOV
(1923-1997)

A Name

When Eve walked among
the animals and named them—
nightingale, red-shouldered hawk,
fiddler crab, fallow deer—
I wonder if she ever wanted
them to speak back, looked into
their wide wonderful eyes and
whispered, *Name me, name me.*

ADA LIMÓN
(b. 1976)

A Name

Ada Limón, b. 1976

When Eve walked among
the animals and named them—
nightingale, red-shouldered hawk,
fiddler crab, fallow deer—
I wonder if she ever wanted
them to speak back, looked into
their wide wonderful eyes and
whispered, *Name me, name me.*

Holly Sears, *Hudson River Explorers*, 2012

from **Coal**

Love is a word, another kind of open.
As the diamond comes
into a knot of flame
I am Black
because I come from the earth's inside
take my word for jewel
in the open light.

AUDRE LORDE
(1934–1992)

The Taxi

When I go away from you
The world beats dead
Like a slackened drum.
I call out for you against the jutted stars
And shout into the ridges of the wind.
Streets coming fast,
One after the other,
Wedge you away from me,
And the lamps of the city prick my eyes
So that I can no longer see your face.
Why should I leave you,
To wound myself upon the sharp edges of the night?

AMY LOWELL
(1874-1925)

A Little Tooth

Your baby grows a tooth, then two,
and four, and five, then she wants some meat
directly from the bone. It's all

over: she'll learn some words, she'll fall
in love with cretins, dolts, a sweet
talker on his way to jail. And you,

your wife, get old, flyblown, and rue
nothing. You did, you loved, your feet
are sore. It's dusk. Your daughter's tall.

THOMAS LUX
(1946–2017)

The Tropics in New York

Bananas ripe and green, and ginger-root,
Cocoa in pods and alligator pears,
And tangerines and mangoes and grape fruit,
Fit for the highest prize at parish fairs,

Set in the window, bringing memories
Of fruit-trees laden by low-singing rills,
And dewy dawns, and mystical blue skies
In benediction over nun-like hills.

My eyes grew dim, and I could no more gaze;
A wave of longing through my body swept,
And, hungry for the old, familiar ways,
I turned aside and bowed my head and wept.

CLAUDE MCKAY
(1889–1948)

A Renewal

Having used every subterfuge
To shake you, lies, fatigue, or even that of passion,
Now I see no way but a clean break.
I add that I am willing to bear the guilt.

You nod assent. Autumn turns windy, huge,
A clear vase of dry leaves vibrating on and on.
We sit, watching. When I next speak
Love buries itself in me, up to the hilt.

JAMES MERRILL
(1926–1995)

Separation

Your absence has gone through me
Like thread through a needle.
Everything I do is stitched with its color.

W. S. MERWIN
(b. 1927)

Travel

The railroad track is miles away,
    And the day is loud with voices speaking,
Yet there isn't a train goes by all day
    But I hear its whistle shrieking.

All night there isn't a train goes by,
    Though the night is still for sleep and dreaming,
But I see its cinders red on the sky,
    And hear its engine steaming.

My heart is warm with the friends I make,
    And better friends I'll not be knowing;
Yet there isn't a train I wouldn't take,
    No matter where it's going.

EDNA ST. VINCENT MILLAY
(1892–1950)

The Gift

For Bobby Jack Nelson

Older, more generous,
We give each other hope.
The gift is ominous:
Enough praise, enough rope.

N. SCOTT MOMADAY
(b. 1934)

from **Love in the Ruins**

I remember my mother toward the end,

folding the tablecloth after dinner
        so carefully,
as if it were the flag
        of a country that no longer existed,
but once had ruled the world.

JIM MOORE
(b. 1943)

John Cavanagh, *Commuting/Community*

from **Love in the Ruins**

I remember my mother toward the end,

folding the tablecloth after dinner
    so carefully,
as if it were the flag
    of a country that no longer existed,
but once had ruled the world.

Jim Moore, b. 1943

The Sonogram

Only a few weeks ago, the sonogram of Jean's womb
resembled nothing so much
as a satellite-map of Ireland:

now the image
is so well-defined we can make out not only a hand
but a thumb;

on the road to Spiddal, a woman hitching a ride;
a gladiator in his net, passing judgement on the crowd.

PAUL MULDOON
(b. 1951)

A Strange Beautiful Woman

A strange beautiful woman
met me in the mirror
the other night.
Hey,
I said,
What you doing here?
She asked me
the same thing.

MARILYN NELSON
(b. 1946)

A Strange Beautiful Woman

Marilyn Nelson, b. 1946

A strange beautiful woman
met me in the mirror
the other night.
Hey,
I said,
What you doing here?
She asked me
the same thing.

Philemona Williamson, *Seasons*, 2007

Wilderness

You are the man
You are my other country
and I find it hard going

You are the prickly pear
You are the sudden violent storm

the torrent to raise the river
to float the wounded doe

LORINE NIEDECKER
(1903–1970)

My Heart

I'm not going to cry all the time
nor shall I laugh all the time,
I don't prefer one "strain" to another.
I'd have the immediacy of a bad movie,
not just a sleeper, but also the big,
overproduced first-run kind. I want to be
at least as alive as the vulgar. And if
some aficionado of my mess says "That's
not like Frank!," all to the good! I
don't wear brown and grey suits all the time,
do I? No. I wear workshirts to the opera,
often. I want my feet to be bare,
I want my face to be shaven, and my heart—
you can't plan on the heart, but
the better part of it, my poetry, is open.

FRANK O'HARA
(1926–1966)

Primitive

I have heard about the civilized,
the marriages run on talk, elegant and
honest, rational. But you and I are
savages. You come in with a bag,
hold it out to me in silence.
I know Moo Shu Pork when I smell it
and understand the message: I have
pleased you greatly last night. We sit
quietly, side by side, to eat,
the long pancakes dangling and spilling,
fragrant sauce dripping out,
and glance at each other askance, wordless,
the corners of our eyes clear as spear points
laid along the sill to show
a friend sits with a friend here.

SHARON OLDS
(b. 1942)

Unfortunate Coincidence

By the time you swear you're his,
   Shivering and sighing,
And he vows his passion is
   Infinite, undying—
Lady, make a note of this:
   One of you is lying.

DOROTHY PARKER
(1893-1967)

If there is something to desire

If there is something to desire,
there will be something to regret.
If there is something to regret,
there will be something to recall.
If there is something to recall,
there was nothing to regret.
If there was nothing to regret,
there was nothing to desire.

VERA PAVLOVA
(b. 1963)
Translated, from the Russian, by Steven Seymour

Brotherhood
Homage to Claudius Ptolemy

I am a man: little do I last
and the night is enormous.
But I look up:
the stars write.
Unknowing I understand:
I too am written,
and at this very moment
someone spells me out.

OCTAVIO PAZ
(1914–1998)
Translated, from the Spanish, by Eliot Weinberger

Heaven

It will be the past
and we'll live there together.

Not as it was *to live*
but as it is remembered.

It will be the past.
We'll all go back together.

Everyone we ever loved,
and lost, and must remember.

It will be the past.
And it will last forever.

PATRICK PHILLIPS
(b. 1970)

HEAVEN

Patrick Phillips b. 1970

It will be the past
and we'll live there together.

Not as it was *to live*
but as it is remembered.

It will be the past.
We'll all go back together.

Everyone we ever loved,
and lost, and must remember.

It will be the past.
And it will last forever.

Poetry in Motion

Mary Temple, *West Wall, East Light, Morning,* 2011

from **I Am Vertical**

But I would rather be horizontal.
I am not a tree with my root in the soil
Sucking up minerals and motherly love
So that each March I may gleam into leaf,
Nor am I the beauty of a garden bed
Attracting my share of Ahs and spectacularly painted,
Unknowing I must soon unpetal.
Compared with me, a tree is immortal
And a flower-head not tall, but more startling,
And I want the one's longevity and the other's daring.

SYLVIA PLATH
(1932–1963)

Wild Orchids

At the foot of a rock, bamboo and orchids,
small furled flowers that hold themselves aloof
from the mist that is everywhere.
You have left newspapers, indolent
quarrels over Sunday-morning coffee
to come to the museum with your lover
and admire these swirls
swept onto paper by an old monk
in less than ten minutes six hundred years ago
depicting the orchid,
which signifies the virtues of the noble man:
reticence, calm, clarity of mind.

KATHA POLLITT
(b. 1949)

In a Station of the Metro

The apparition of these faces in the crowd:
Petals on a wet, black bough.

EZRA POUND
(1885–1972)

Delta

If you have taken this rubble for my past
raking though it for fragments you could sell
know that I long ago moved on
deeper into the heart of the matter

If you think you can grasp me, think again:
my story flows in more than one direction
a delta springing from the riverbed
with its five fingers spread

ADRIENNE RICH
(1929–2012)

The Sloth

In moving-slow he has no Peer.
You ask him something in his Ear,
He thinks about it for a Year;

And, then, before he says a Word
There, upside down (unlike a Bird),
He will assume that you have Heard—

A most Ex-as-per-at-ing Lug.
But should you call his manner Smug,
He'll sigh and give his Branch a Hug;

Then off again to Sleep he goes,
Still swaying gently by his Toes,
And you just *know* he knows he knows.

THEODORE ROETHKE
(1908–1963)

Voyager

I have become an orchid
washed in on the salt white beach.
Memory,
what can I make of it now
that might please you—
this life, already wasted
and still strewn with
miracles?

MARY RUEFLE
(b. 1952)

Francesco Simeti
Bensonhurst Gardens

Voyager

I have become an orchid
washed in on the salt white beach.
Memory,
what can I make of it now
that might please you—
this life, already wasted
and still strewn with
miracles?

Mary Ruefle b.1952

Out beyond ideas of wrongdoing and rightdoing

Out beyond ideas of wrongdoing and rightdoing,
there is a field. I'll meet you there.

When the soul lies down in that grass,
the world is too full to talk about.
Ideas, language, even the phrase *each other*
doesn't make any sense.

JALAL AL-DIN RUMI
(1207–1273)
Translated, from the Persian, by Coleman Barks and
John Moyne

Dew

As neatly as peas
in their green canoe,
as discreetly as beads
strung in a row,
sit drops of dew
along a blade of grass.
But unattached and
subject to their weight,
they slip if they accumulate.
Down the green tongue
out of the morning sun
into the general damp,
they're gone.

KAY RYAN
(b. 1945)

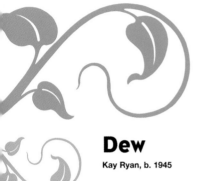

Dew

Kay Ryan, b. 1945

As neatly as peas
in their green canoe,
as discreetly as beads
strung in a row,
sit drops of dew
along a blade of grass.
But unattached and
subject to their weight,
they slip if they accumulate.
Down the green tongue
out of the morning sun
into the general damp,
they're gone.

Joy Taylor, *Jan Peeck's Vine*, 2012

You Say, "I Will Come."

You say, "I will come."
And you do not come.
Now you say, "I will not come."
So I shall expect you.
Have I learned to understand you?

LADY ŌTOMO NO SAKANOE
(c. 700–750)
Translated, from the Japanese, by Kenneth Rexroth

A Poem for Jesse

your face like
summer lightning
gets caught in my voice
and i draw you up from
deep rivers
taste your face of a
thousand names
see you smile
a new season
hear your voice
a wild sea pausing in the wind.

(b. 1934)

Thank You, My Dear

Thank you, my dear

You came, and you did
well to come: I needed
you. You have made

love blaze up in
my breast—bless you!
Bless you as often

as the hours have
been endless to me
while you were gone

SAPPHO
(c. 600 BC)
Translated, from the Greek, by Mary Barnard

What Do You Believe A Poem Shd Do?

quite simply a
poem shd fill you
up with something/
cd make you swoon,
stop in yr tracks,
change yr mind,
or make it up.
a poem shd happen
to you like cold
water or a kiss.

NTOZAKE SHANGE
(b. 1948)

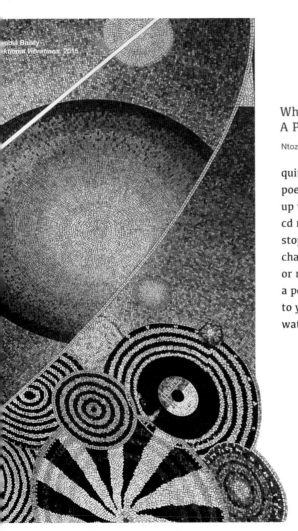

What Do You Believe A Poem Shd Do?

Ntozake Shange b.1948

quite simply a
poem shd fill you
up with something/
cd make you swoon,
stop in yr tracks,
change yr mind,
or make it up.
a poem shd happen
to you like cold
water or a kiss.

Poem Charles Simic, b. 1938

Every morning I forget how it is.
I watch the smoke mount
In great strides above the city.
I belong to no one.

Then I remember my shoes,
How I have to put them on,
How bending over to tie them up
I will look into the earth.

Derek Lerner, *AVEX3(station)*, 2016

Poem

Every morning I forget how it is.
I watch the smoke mount
In great strides above the city.
I belong to no one.

Then I remember my shoes,
How I have to put them on,
How bending over to tie them up
I will look into the earth.

CHARLES SIMIC
(b. 1938)

The Good Life

When some people talk about money
They speak as if it were a mysterious lover
Who went out to buy milk and never
Came back, and it makes me nostalgic
For the years I lived on coffee and bread,
Hungry all the time, walking to work on payday
Like a woman journeying for water
From a village without a well, then living
One or two nights like everyone else
On roast chicken and red wine.

TRACY K. SMITH
(b. 1972)

Amy Bennett
Heydays

The Good Life

When some people talk about money
They speak as if it were a mysterious lover
Who went out to buy milk and never
Came back, and it makes me nostalgic
For the years I lived on coffee and bread,
Hungry all the time, walking to work on payday
Like a woman journeying for water
From a village without a well, then living
One or two nights like everyone else
On roast chicken and red wine.

Tracy K. Smith b. 1972

Here

Gary Snyder, b. 1930

In the dark
(The new moon long set)

A soft grumble in the breeze
Is the sound of a jet so high
It's already long gone by

Some planet
Rising from the east   shines
Through the trees

It's been years since I thought,

Why are we here?

30. VIII. 09

Here

In the dark
(The new moon long set)

A soft grumble in the breeze
Is the sound of a jet so high
It's already long gone by

Some planet
Rising from the east   shines
Through the trees

It's been years since I thought,

Why are we here?

GARY SNYDER
(b. 1930)

Keeping Things Whole

In a field
I am the absence
of field.
This is
always the case.
Wherever I am
I am what is missing.

When I walk
I part the air
and always
the air moves in
to fill the spaces
where my body's been.

We all have reasons
for moving.
I move
to keep things whole.

MARK STRAND
(1934–2014)

Four in the Morning

The hour from night to day.
The hour from side to side.
The hour for those past thirty.

The hour swept clean to the crowing of cocks.
The hour when earth betrays us.
The hour when wind blows from extinguished stars.
The hour of and-what-if-nothing-remains-after-us.

The hollow hour.
Blank, empty.
The very pit of all other hours.

No one feels good at four in the morning.
If ants feel good at four in the morning
—three cheers for the ants. And let five o'clock come
if we're to go on living.

WISŁAWA SZYMBORSKA
(1923–2012)
*Translated, from the Polish, by Magnus J. Krynski and
Robert A. Maguire*

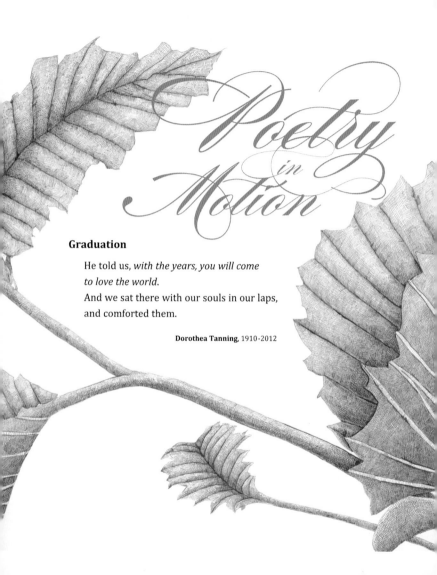

Poetry in Motion

Graduation

He told us, *with the years, you will come*
to love the world.
And we sat there with our souls in our laps,
and comforted them.

Dorothea Tanning, 1910-2012

Graduation

He told us, *with the years, you will come
to love the world.*
And we sat there with our souls in our laps,
and comforted them.

DOROTHEA TANNING
(1910–2012)

The Eagle

He clasps the crag with crookèd hands;
Close to the sun in lonely lands,
Ringed with the azure world, he stands.

The wrinkled sea beneath him crawls;
He watches from his mountain walls,
And like a thunderbolt he falls.

ALFRED, LORD TENNYSON
(1809–1892)

Espresso

Black coffee at sidewalk cafés
with chairs and tables like gaudy insects.

It is a precious sip we intercept
filled with the same strength as Yes and No.

It is fetched out of gloomy kitchens
and looks into the sun without blinking.

In daylight a dot of wholesome black
quickly drained by the wan patron . . .

Like those black drops of profundity
sometimes absorbed by the soul

that give us a healthy push: Go!
The courage to open our eyes.

TOMAS TRANSTRÖMER
(1931–2015)
*Translated, from the Swedish, by May Swenson with
Leif Sjöberg*

To the Reader: Twilight

Whenever I look
out at the snowy
mountains at this hour
and speak directly
into the ear of the sky,
it's you I'm thinking of.
You're like the spirits
the children invent
to inhabit the stuffed horse
and the doll.
I don't know who hears me.
I don't know who speaks
when the horse speaks.

CHASE TWICHELL
(b. 1950)

To the Reader:
Twilight

Whenever I look
out at the snowy
mountains at this hour
and speak directly
into the ear of the sky,
it's you I'm thinking of.
You're like the spirits
the children invent
to inhabit the stuffed horse
and the doll.
I don't know who hears me.
I don't know who speaks
when the horse speaks.

Chase Twichell b.1950

Poetry in Motion

Felipe Galindo
Magic Realism in Kingsbridge

Exile

The widow refuses sleep, for sleep pretends
that it can bring him back.
In this way,
the will is set against the appetite.
Even the empty hand moves to the mouth.
Apart from you,
I turn a corner in the city and find,
for a moment, the old climate,
the little blue flower everywhere.

ELLEN BRYANT VOIGT
(b. 1943)

Star

If, in the light of things, you fade
real, yet wanly withdrawn
to our determined and appropriate
distance, like the moon left on
all night among the leaves, may
you invisibly delight this house,
O star, doubly compassionate, who came
too soon for twilight, too late
for dawn, may your faint flame
strive with the worst in us
through chaos
with the passion of
plain day.

DEREK WALCOTT
(b. 1930–2017)

Lineage

My grandmothers were strong.
They followed plows and bent to toil.
They moved through fields sowing seed.
They touched earth and grain grew.
They were full of sturdiness and singing.
My grandmothers were strong.

My grandmothers are full of memories
Smelling of soap and onions and wet clay
With veins rolling roughly over quick hands
They have many clean words to say.
My grandmothers were strong.
Why am I not as they?

MARGARET WALKER
(1915–1998)

from **Crossing Brooklyn Ferry**

Flood-tide below me! I see you face to face!
Clouds of the west—sun there half an hour high—I see you
    also face to face.
Crowds of men and women attired in the usual costumes,
    how curious you are to me!
On the ferry-boats the hundreds and hundreds that cross,
    returning home, are more curious to me than you suppose,
And you that shall cross from shore to shore years hence are more
    to me, and more in my meditations, than you might suppose.

WALT WHITMAN
(1819–1892)

Transit

A woman I have never seen before
Steps from the darkness of her town-house door
At just that crux of time when she is made
So beautiful that she or time must fade.

What use to claim that as she tugs her gloves
A phantom heraldry of all the loves
Blares from the lintel? That the staggered sun
Forgets, in his confusion, how to run?

Still, nothing changes as her perfect feet
Click down the walk that issues in the street,
Leaving the stations of her body there
As a whip maps the countries of the air.

RICHARD WILBUR
(b. 1921)

This Is Just to Say

I have eaten
the plums
that were in
the icebox

and which
you were probably
saving
for breakfast

Forgive me
they were delicious
so sweet
and so cold

WILLIAM CARLOS WILLIAMS
(1883–1963)

Let No Charitable Hope

Now let no charitable hope
Confuse my mind with images
Of eagle and of antelope:
I am in nature none of these.

I was, being human, born alone;
I am, being woman, hard beset;
I live by squeezing from a stone
The little nourishment I get.

In masks outrageous and austere
The years go by in single file;
But none has merited my fear,
And none has quite escaped my smile.

ELINOR WYLIE
(1885–1928)

west of rest is sleep
east, dream
where waters meet
north, emptiness,
south, wakefulness,
and out, rising up
to the stars, peace

JEFFREY YANG
(b. 1974)

Poetry in Motion

west of rest is sleep
east, dream
where waters meet
north, emptiness,
south, wakefulness,
and out, rising up
to the stars, peace

Jeffrey Yang, *b.1974*

Holly Sears, *Hudson River Explorer*

When You are Old

When you are old and grey and full of sleep,
And nodding by the fire, take down this book,
And slowly read, and dream of the soft look
Your eyes had once, and of their shadows deep;

How many loved your moments of glad grace,
And loved your beauty with love false or true,
But one man loved the pilgrim soul in you,
And loved the sorrows of your changing face;

And bending down beside the glowing bars,
Murmur, a little sadly, how Love fled
And paced upon the mountains overhead
And hid his face amid a crowd of stars.

W. B. YEATS
(1865–1939)

Ragtime

Like hot food
I love you

like warm
bread & cold

cuts, butter
sammiches

or, days later, after
Thanksgiving

when I want
whatever's left

KEVIN YOUNG
(b. 1970)

Raul Colón, *Primavera*

Ragtime

Like hot food
I love you

like warm
bread & cold

cuts, butter
sammiches

or, days later, after
Thanksgiving

when I want
whatever's left

Kevin Young, b. 1970

Just Children
For Ewunia

It was just children playing in the sand
(accompanied by the narcotic scent
of blooming lindens, don't forget),
just children, but after all
the devil, and the minor gods,
and even forgotten politicians,
who'd broken all their promises,
were also there and watched them
with unending rapture.
Who wouldn't want to be a child
—for the last time!

ADAM ZAGAJEWSKI
(b. 1945)
Translated, from the Polish, by Clare Cavanagh

Notes on the Poets

Anna Akhmatova (1889–1966) is one of the most acclaimed writers in the Russian canon. During her life, her work was often censored, and she faced persecution from the Stalinist authorities. Her many collections include (in translation) *Rosary*, *White Flock*, *Requiem*, *The Flight of Time*, and *Selected Poems*.

Elizabeth Alexander (1962–), the author of two books of essays, six collections of poems including *American Sublime* (2005), a finalist for the Pulitzer Prize, and the memoir *The Light of the World* (2015), also a Pulitzer finalist, composed and delivered the poem "Praise Song for the Day" for the 2009 inauguration of President Barack Obama.

Maya Angelou (1928–2014) was the author of more than a dozen books, including the memoir *I Know Why the Caged Bird Sings* (1969), the collection of poems *Just Give Me a Cool Drink of Water 'fore I Diiie* (1971), nominated for the Pulitzer Prize, and *The Complete Collected Poems of Maya Angelou* (1994).

W. H. Auden (1907–1973) was an English-born poet who became a U.S. citizen after he moved to New York in 1939. His books include *The Age of Anxiety* (1947), which won the Pulitzer Prize, *The Shield of Achilles* (1955), and *Collected Poems*, edited by Edward Mendelson (1976).

Ingeborg Bachmann (1926–1973), Austrian writer, is the author of the story collection *The Thirtieth Year* (1961; translated by Michael Bullock, 1964), *Last Living Words: The Ingeborg Bachmann Reader* (translated by Lilian M. Friedberg, 2005), and *Darkness Spoken: The Collected Poems* (translated by Peter Filkins, 2005).

Elizabeth Bishop (1911–1979), is the author of *Poems: North & South—A Cold Spring* (1955), winner of the Pulitzer Prize, *Questions of Travel* (1965), *The Complete Poems* (1969), winner of the National Book Award, and *Geography III* (1976). New centennial editions of her work, *Poems* and *Prose* (edited by Lloyd Schwartz), were published in 2011.

William Blake (1757–1827), master engraver, illustrator, and poet, was the author of some fifteen major works, including *Poetical Studies* (1783), *Songs of Innocence* (1789), *Songs of Experience* (1794), and *Visions of the Daughters of Albion* (1793).

Anne Bradstreet (1612–1672) was the author of *The Tenth Muse, Lately Sprung Up in America*, published in England in 1650 and the only book of hers to appear in her lifetime. *Several Poems Compiled with Great Wit and Learning* appeared in America in 1678.

Gwendolyn Brooks (1917–2000), Poetry Consultant to the Library of Congress (1985), Illinois Poet Laureate (1968–2000), author of *A Street in Bronzeville* (1945), and winner of the Pulitzer Prize for *Annie Allen* (1949), also wrote *Maud Martha*, a novel (1953), and *Blacks* (1987).

Nina Cassian (1924–2014) was a Romanian-born poet and composer who took up residence in New York in the 1980s. Her English-language collections include *Life Sentence: Selected Poems* (1990), *Take My Word for It* (1998), and *Continuum* (2008), and she wrote fiction, books for children, and essays as well.

Ana Castillo (1953–) is a poet, essayist, novelist, and translator, author of collections including *My Father was a Toltec and Selected Poems 1973–1988* (1995) and *I Ask The Impossible* (2001) as well as *My Mother's Mexico: New and Collected Essays* (2015).

Marilyn Chin (1955–) grew up in Oregon after her family emigrated from Hong Kong. Her many award-winning books include *The Phoenix Gone, The Terrace Empty* (1994), *Rhapsody in Plain Yellow* (2003), *Revenge of the Mooncake Vixen* (2009), and *Hard Love Province* (2014).

Chu Chen Po (9th century). This version of "Hedgehog" by the prolific translator and poet Kenneth Rexroth was published in *Love and the Turning Year: One Hundred More Poems from the Chinese* (1970). *The Complete Poems of Kenneth Rexroth* was published in 2003.

Sandra Cisneros (1954–) is the author of the novel *The House on Mango Street* (1984) and collections of poems, including *My Wicked, Wicked Ways* (1987) and *Loose Woman* (1994) as well as *Woman Hollering Creek and Other Stories* (1991). She was awarded a MacArthur Foundation Fellowship in 1995.

Lucille Clifton (1936–2010), Poetry Society of America Frost Medalist, is the author of *Good Woman: Poems and a Memoir, 1969–1980* and *Next: New Poems*, both short-listed for the Pulitzer Prize in 1987, the National Book Award winner *Blessing the Boats: New and Selected Poems, 1988–2000*, and *The Collected Poems of Lucille Clifton 1965–2010*, edited by Kevin Young and Michael S. Glaser.

Billy Collins (1941–) served as U.S. Poet Laureate (2001–3) and New York State Poet Laureate (2004–6). A Guggenheim Fellow, he is the author of many books including *Picnic, Lightning* (1998), *Sailing Alone Around the Room: New and Selected Poems* (2001), *Ballistics* (2008), and *Aimless Love* (2013).

Sor Juana Inés de la Cruz (1651–1695), a self-taught intellectual, court favorite, and nun rising to prominence in Mexico City during the Spanish Golden Age (and called the "Tenth Muse" and the "Phoenix of Mexico") is the author of *The Trials of a Noble House* (1683), *The Divine Narcissus* (1692), and others.

Emily Dickinson (1830–1886) has been regarded as a major figure in American poetry since 1955 when the Belknap Press of Harvard University published the first comprehensive edition of her work, edited by Thomas H. Johnson and including 1,775 poems in three volumes.

Rita Dove (1952–), Poet Laureate of the United States from 1993 to 1995, received the National Humanities Medal in 1996 and the National Medal of the Arts in 2011. Her books include *Thomas and Beulah*, winner of the 1987 Pulitzer Prize, *American Smooth* (2004), and *Collected Poems, 1974–2004*.

Paul Laurence Dunbar (1872–1906) is the author of *Majors and Minors* and *Lyrics of Lowly Life* (1896), *When Malindy Sings* and *Lyrics of Love and Laughter* (1903), *Complete Poems* (1913), and *The Best Stories of Paul Laurence Dunbar* (1938).

T. S. Eliot (1888–1965) received the 1948 Nobel Prize in Literature. Born in Missouri, he settled in England in 1914 and was for most of his life an editor at Faber & Faber. His books include *Prufrock and Other Observations* (1917), *The Waste Land* (1922), *Four Quartets* (1943), and *Collected Poems, 1909–1935*.

Louise Erdrich (1954–) has published three books of poems, *Jacklight* (1984), *Baptism of Desire* (1989), and *Original Fire: Selected and New Poems* (2003) as well as novels and collections of stories for which she received the PEN/Saul Bellow Award for Achievement in American Fiction in 2014.

James Fenton (1949–) is the author of many books, including *A German Requiem* (1981), *Out of Danger* (1994), *Leonardo's Nephew: Essays on Art and Artists* (1998), *The Strength of Poetry: Oxford Lectures* (2001), and *Selected Poems* (2006). He has received the Queen's Gold Medal for Poetry and the PEN Pinter Prize.

Lawrence Ferlinghetti (1919–), central to the cultural renaissance known as the Beat movement, is the publisher of City Lights Books. His collections include *A Coney Island of the Mind* (1958), *A Far Rockaway of the Heart* (1997), and *How to Paint Sunlight: Lyric Poems & Others, 1997–2000*.

Robert Frost (1874–1963) was awarded the Pulitzer Prize four times and the Gold Medal from the Poetry Society of America in 1941. The Library of America's *Robert Frost: Collected Poems, Prose, and Plays*, edited by Richard Poirier and Mark Richardson, was published in 1995.

Tess Gallagher (1943–) is the author of many collections, including *Instructions to the Double* (1976) and *Midnight Lantern: New and Selected Poems* (2011) as well as *The Lover of Horses and Other Stories* (1986), *At the Owl Woman Saloon* (1997), and *The Man from Kinvara: Selected Stories* (2009).

Federico García Lorca (1898–1936), poet and dramatist, is the author of *Gypsy Ballads* (1928), *Poet in New York* (1929), *The Selected Poems of Federico García Lorca,* newly translated by Pablo Medina and Mark Statman (2007), and the play *Blood Wedding* (1932).

Nikki Giovanni (1943–) is the author of *The Collected Poetry of Nikki Giovanni: 1968–1998, Acolytes* (2007), *Bicycles: Love Poems* (2009), *and Chasing Utopia: A Hybrid* (2013) as well as many books for children. She has been awarded twenty honorary degrees from colleges and universities.

Aracelis Girmay (1977–) has published *Teeth* (2007), *Kingdom Animalia* (2011), winner of the Isabella Gardner Poetry Award and a finalist for the National Book Critics Circle Award, and *The Black Maria* (2016). A Cave Canem Fellow, she received a Whiting Award in 2015.

Louise Glück (1943–) was U.S. Poet Laureate in 2003. Her books include *The Wild Iris* (1992), winner of the Pulitzer Prize, *Vita Nova* (1999), winner of the Bollingen Prize, *Poems: 1962–2012, Faithful and Virtuous Night* (2014), winner of the National Book Award, and *American Originality: Essays on Poetry* (2017).

Nathalie Handal (1969–) is the author of *The Neverfield* (1999), *The Lives of Rain* (2005), *Love and Strange Horses* (2010), and *Poet in Andalucía* (2012). Her many honors include a Lannan Fellowship and the Alejo Zuloaga Order in Literature.

Joy Harjo (1951–) winner of the 2015 Wallace Stevens Award and many others, is the author of *A Map to the Next World: Poetry and Tales* (2000), *How We Became Human: New and Selected Poems 1975–2002*, the memoir *Crazy Brave* (2012), winner of an American Book Award, and *Conflict Resolution for Holy Beings* (2015).

Robert Hayden (1913–1980), Consultant in Poetry to the Library of Congress (1976–78), is the author of *Figure of Time: Poems* (1955) as well as *Robert Hayden: Collected Prose* (1984) and *Robert Hayden: Collected Poems* (1985), both edited by Frederick Glaysher.

Seamus Heaney (1939–2013), awarded the 1995 Nobel Prize in Literature, is the author of many collections of poems and essays, including *Death of a Naturalist* (1966), *North* (1975), *The Haw Lantern* (1987), *Opened Ground: Selected Poems, 1966–1996 (1998), District and Circle*, winner of the 2006 T. S. Eliot Prize, and *Finders Keepers: Selected Prose, 1971–2001.*

Lance Henson (1944–) began his career with *Keeper of Arrows* (1971), followed by many collections including *Le Orme de Tasso/The Badger Tracks* (1989), *A Cheyenne Sketchbook: Selected Poems, 1970–1991*, *A Motion of Sudden Aloneness: Expatriate Songs* (1991), and *Paria* (2004).

Gerard Manley Hopkins (1844–1889) published very little in his lifetime. *Poems of Gerard Manley Hopkins*, edited by Robert Bridges, was issued in 1918, his *Notebooks and Papers* in 1937, several volumes of correspondence in 1955, and *Sermons and Devotional Writings* in 1959.

Fanny Howe (1940–) has published more than twenty books including novels and books for young adults. Her *Selected Poems* (2000) won the Lenore Marshall Poetry Prize. She was also awarded the Ruth Lilly Poetry Prize in 2009 and in 2014, her *Second Childhood* was a National Book Award finalist.

Langston Hughes (1902–1967), a major figure of the Harlem Renaissance, wrote stories, novels, and plays as well as collections of poems including *The Weary Blues* (1926), *Fields of Wonder* (1947), *Montage of a Dream Deferred* (1951), and (published posthumously) *The Collected Poems* (1994), edited by Arnold Rampersad.

Ted Hughes (1930–1998), translator, essayist, editor, and Poet Laureate of England from 1984 until his death, is the author of *The Hawk in the Rain* (1957), *Crow* (1970), *Selected Poems, 1957–1981*, *Winter Pollen: Occasional Prose* (1994), and *The Birthday Letters* (1998). His *Collected Poems*, edited by Paul Keegan, was published in 2003.

Kobayashi Issa (1763–1828), haiku poet, is also the author of prose, including *Journal of My Father's Last Day* and *The Year of My Life*. Robert Hass, translator, was U.S. Poet Laureate from 1995 to 1997 and won both the Pulitzer Prize and the National Book Award for *Time and Materials: Poems, 1997–2005*.

Major Jackson (1968–) is the author of *Leaving Saturn* (2002), winner of the Cave Canem Poetry Prize and a finalist for the National Book Critics Circle Award, *Hoops* (2006) and *Holding Company* (2010), both finalists for an NAACP Image Award, and *Roll Deep* (2015). He is poetry editor of *The Harvard Review*.

John Keats (1795–1821), English Romantic poet, published in his lifetime *Poems* (1817), *Endymion: A Poetic Romance* (1818), and *Lamia, Isabella, The Eve of St. Agnes, and Other Poems* (1820). *The Poetical Works of John Keats* was first published in America in 1846 and *The Letters of John Keats* in 1958.

Jane Kenyon (1947–1995), a translator of Anna Akhmatova, is the author of *From Room to Room* (1978), *The Boat of Quiet Hours* (1986), *Let Evening Come* (1990), *Constance* (1993), the posthumously published *Otherwise: New & Selected Poems* (1996), and *Collected Poems* (2007).

Galway Kinnell (1927–2014) won the Pulitzer Prize and the National Book Award for his *Selected Poems* (1982). From 1989 to 1993, he was Poet Laureate of Vermont. His books include *The Book of Nightmares* (1971), *Imperfect Thirst* (1994), *A New Selected Poems* (2001), and *Strong Is Your Hold* (2006).

Kenneth Koch (1925–2002) wrote many books including *Wishes, Lies, and Dreams: Teaching Children to Write Poetry* (1970), *One Thousand Avant-Garde Plays* (1988), *One Train: Poems* and *On the Great Atlantic Rainway: Selected Poems, 1950–1988*, together awarded the Bollingen Prize in 1995, and *New Addresses* (2000).

Ted Kooser (1939–) was awarded the Pulitzer Prize for his collection *Delights and Shadows* in 2004, the year he became U.S. Poet Laureate. Other books include *Sure Signs* (1980), *Flying at Night: Poems, 1965–1985* (2005), and *The Poetry Home Repair Manual: Practical Advice for Beginning Poets* (2005).

Stanley Kunitz (1905–2006) was named U.S. Poet Laureate in 2000 at the age of ninety-five. His books include *Intellectual Things* (1930), *Passport to War* (1944), *Selected Poems: 1928–1958*, which won the Pulitzer Prize, *The Testing-Tree* (1971), and *The Collected Poems of Stanley Kunitz* (2000).

Li-Young Lee (1957–), winner of the Delmore Schwartz Memorial Award for *Rose* (1986), the Lamont Poetry Prize for *The City in Which I Love You* (1990), and an American Book Award for *The Winged Seed: A Remembrance* (1995), has also written *Behind My Eyes* (2009) and *The Word from His Song* (2016).

Denise Levertov (1923–1997), essayist, translator, and poet, is the author of *O Taste and See: New Poems* (1964), *The Freeing of the Dust* (1975), winner of the Lenore Marshall Prize, *Poems: 1968–1972* (1987), and (published posthumously) *This Great Unknowing: Last Poems* (1999).

Ada Limón (1976–), winner of the Chicago Literary Award for Poetry, was a finalist for both the National Book Award and the National Book Critics Circle Award for her collection *Bright Dead Things* (2015). She is also the author of *This Big Fake World* (2006), *Lucky Wreck* (2006), and *Sharks on the Rivers* (2010).

Audre Lorde (1934–1992), New York State Poet from 1991 to 1993, is the author of *The Black Unicorn* (1978), *Chosen Poems Old and New* (1982), and (published posthumously) *The Collected Poems of Audre Lorde* (1997), as well as *The Cancer Journals* (1980) and *Need: A Chorale for Black Women Voices* (1990).

Amy Lowell (1874–1925), winner (posthumously) of the 1926 Pulitzer Prize for *What's O'Clock*, edited *Some Imagist Poets: An Anthology* (1915) and wrote *Tendencies in Modern American Poetry* in 1917. *Amy Lowell: Selected Poems*, edited by Honor Moore, was published in 2004.

Thomas Lux (1946–2017), winner of the Kingsley Tufts Award for his collection *Split Horizon* (1994), is also the author of *Memory's Handgrenade* (1972), *Sunday: Poems* (1979), *New and Selected Poems, 1975–1995* (1997), *The Street of Clocks* (2001), *God Particles* (2008), and *To the Left of Time* (2016).

Claude McKay (1889–1948), a key figure of the Harlem Renaissance, wrote *Songs of Jamaica* and *Constab Ballads* (both 1912), *Spring in New Hampshire and Other Poems* (1920), the novels *Home to Harlem* (1928) and *Banana Bottom* (1933), and essays collected in *Harlem: Negro Metropolis* (1940).

James Merrill (1926–1995), awarded the National Book Award for *Nights and Days* (1966) and *Mirabell: Books of Number* (1978), the Pulitzer Prize for *Divine Comedies* (1976), and the National Book Critics Circle Award for *The Changing Light at Sandover* (1982), published *Recitative: Prose* in 1986 and his memoir *A Different Person* in 1993.

W. S. Merwin (1927–), winner of the Bollingen Prize (1979), the Pulitzer Prize for both *The Carrier of Ladders* (1970) and *The Shadow of Sirius* (2008), and the National Book Award for *Migration: New and Selected Poems* (2005), is the author of more than thirty books and a prolific translator and memoirist.

Edna St. Vincent Millay (1892–1950) published her debut collection *Renascence and Other Poems* in 1917. She won the Pulitzer Prize in 1922 for *The Ballad of the Harp-Weaver: A Few Figs from Thistles: 8 Sonnets in American Poetry*. A new edition of her *Collected Poems*, edited by Holly Peppe, was published in 2011.

N. Scott Momaday (1934–) won the Pulitzer Prize for his debut novel *House Made of Dawn* (1969). His poems are collected in *The Gourd Dancer* (1976), *In the Bear's House* (1999), and *In the Presence of the Sun: Stories and Poems, 1961–1991*. His children's book *Circle of Wonder* was published in 1994.

Jim Moore (1943–), recipient of fellowships from the Guggenheim and the McKnight Foundations, is the author of *The New Body* (1976), *The Freedom of History* (1988), *The Long Experience of Love* (1995), *Lightning at Dinner* (2005), *Invisible Strings* (2011), and *Underground: New and Selected Poems* (2014).

Paul Muldoon (1951–), poet, translator, musician, and poetry editor of *The New Yorker* (2007–17), is the author of many books, including *New Weather* (1973), *The Annals of Chile* (1995), *Moy Sand and Gravel* (2002), winner of both the Pulitzer and the International Griffin Poetry Prize, and *Selected Poems 1968–2014* (2016).

Marilyn Nelson (1946–) is the author of *The Homeplace* (1990), *The Fields of Praise: New and Selected Poems* (1997), and *Carver: A Life in Poems* (2001), all finalists for the National Book Award. She was awarded the Frost Medal from the Poetry Society of America and the Neustadt Prize for Children's Literature.

Lorine Niedecker (1903–1970) published few books in her lifetime—among them *New Goose* (1946), *My Friend Tree* (1962), *North Central* (1968), and *T & G: The Collected Poems 1936–1966* (1969). Important volumes have appeared since, most notably *Lorine Niedecker: Collected Works* (2002), edited by Jenny Penberthy, and *Lake Superior* (2013).

Frank O'Hara (1926–1966) published his poems in small (and now very rare) editions and in two famous collections, *Meditations in an Emergency* (1957) and *Lunch Poems* (1965). After his death, *The Collected Poems of Frank O'Hara*, edited by Donald Allen (1971), received the National Book Award. A new *Selected Poems,* edited by Mark Ford, was published in 2009.

Sharon Olds (1942–) began her career with *Satan Says* (1980), followed by *The Dead and the Living* (1984), which won the National Book Critics Circle Award, later also bestowed upon *Strike Sparks: Selected Poems, 1980–2002* (2004). *Stag's Leap* (2012) was awarded both the Pulitzer and the T. S. Eliot Prize.

Dorothy Parker (1893–1967) was a contributor to *The New Yorker* from its earliest days. Her books of poems, *Enough Rope* (1926), *Death and Taxes* (1931), and *Collected Poems: Not So Deep as a Well* (1936), were hugely popular, as were the stories collected in *Laments for the Living* (1930).

Vera Pavlova (1963–) was born in Moscow. She is the author of twenty collections of poetry, and her work has been translated into twenty-two languages. Steven Seymour translated her collection *If There Is Something to Desire* (2011) as well as *Album for the Young (and Old): Poems* (2017).

Octavio Paz (1914–1998) won the Nobel Prize in Literature in 1990. His first book, *The Labyrinth of Solitude: Life and Thought in Mexico*, was published in 1950, and *The Poems of Octavio Paz*, edited and translated by Eliot Weinberger (with additional translations by others), was issued in 2012.

Patrick Phillips (1970–), a translator of the poems of Henrik Nordbrandt and a Guggenheim Fellow, is the author of *Chattahoochee* (2004), winner of the Kate Tufts Discovery Award, *Boy* (2008), *Elegy for a Broken Machine* (2015), and *Blood at the Root: A Racial Cleansing in America* (2016).

Sylvia Plath (1932–1963) is the author of the collection *The Colossus* (1960), the novel *The Bell Jar* (1963), and (published posthumously) *Ariel* (1965). Other books include *The Collected Poems of Sylvia Plath*, edited by Ted Hughes (1981), and *The Unabridged Journals of Sylvia Plath, 1950–1962*, edited by Karen V. Kukil (2000).

Katha Pollitt (1949–), longtime columnist for *The Nation* and author of three collections of essays including *Learning to Drive: And Other Life Stories* (2007), received the National Book Critics Circle Award for her debut collection of poems, *Antarctic Traveller* (1981), followed by *The Mind-Body Problem* (2009).

Ezra Pound (1885–1972), translator, critic, poet, and a central force in the "Imagisme" movement in the twentieth century, is the author of *Personae: The Collected Poems* (1926), *Homage to Sextus Propertius* (1934), *The Cantos* (1948), and (published posthumously) *Ezra Pound: Poems and Translations* (2004).

Adrienne Rich (1929–2012), award-winning poet and essayist, is the author of more than twenty-five books, including *A Change of World* (1951), chosen by W. H. Auden for the Yale Series of Younger Poets prize, *Diving into the Wreck: Poems, 1971–1972*, and *On Lies, Secrets, and Silence: Selected Prose, 1966–1978*.

Theodore Roethke (1908–1963) won the Pulitzer Prize for his collection *The Waking: Poems, 1933–1953* and the National Book Award for both *Words for the Wind: The Collected Verse of Theodore Roethke* (1958) and *The Far Field* (1964). *Selected Poems*, edited by Edward Hirsch, was published in 2005.

Mary Ruefle (1952–), a Guggenheim Fellow, has received a Whiting Award and an award from the American Academy of Arts and Letters. Her books include *Selected Poems* (2010), winner of the William Carlos Williams Award, *Madness, Rack, and Honey: Collected Lectures* (2012), and *My Private Property* (2016).

Jalal al-Din Rumi (1207–1273) became a poet while inspired by the mystic Shams-i-Tabrizi. Versions of his work made by Coleman Barks (with John Moyne)—among them *The Essential Rumi* (1995) and *The Illuminated Rumi* (1997)—are the focus of a PBS feature by Bill Moyers in his series *The Language of Life*.

Kay Ryan (1945–), U.S. Poet Laureate, 2008–10, a MacArthur and Guggenheim Fellow, and the recipient of the Ruth Lilly Poetry Prize, is the author of *Flamingo Watching* (1994), *Elephant Rocks* (1996), *The Niagara River* (2005), *The Best of It: New and Selected Poems* (2010), and *Erratic Facts* (2015).

Lady Ōtomo No Sakanoe (c. 700–750) was a leading poet of the Nara period with seventy-nine poems in the *Man'yōshū*, the oldest existing collection of Japanese poetry. Her work can be found in *Woman Poets of Japan*, translated and edited by Kenneth Rexroth and Ikuko Atsumi (1977), and other anthologies.

Sonia Sanchez (1934–) is the author of more than a dozen books including *Does Your House Have Lions?* (1995), *Shake Loose My Skin: New and Selected Poems* (1999), and *Morning Haiku* (2010). Among her many honors are the Robert Creeley Award and the Frost Medal from the Poetry Society of America.

Sappho (c. 600 BC), a composer and performer of songs and one of the greatest poets of world literature, is said to have composed nine books of lyrics although only one poem has survived in its entirety. Anne Carson presents all the surviving fragments in *If Not, Winter* (2002) in Greek and English.

Ntozake Shange (1948–), celebrated author of the play *For Colored Girls Who Have Considered Suicide/When the Rainbow Is Enuf* (1975), has also written novels and books of poems, including *Nappy Edges* (1978) and *Some Men* (1981) along with *See No Evil: Prefaces, Essays & Accounts, 1976–1983*.

Charles Simic (1938–), U.S. Poet Laureate (2007) and a MacArthur Fellow, is the author of more than sixty books including *The World Doesn't End: Prose Poems* (1989), winner of the Pulitzer Prize, *Selected Poems, 1963–2003*, winner of the Griffin International Prize, and *A Fly in the Soup: Memoirs* (2000).

Tracy K. Smith (1972–) is the author of the memoir *Ordinary Light* (2015) and three collections of poems, *The Body's Question* (2003), winner of the Cave Canem First Book Prize, *Duende* (2007), winner of the James Laughlin Award, and *Life on Mars* (2011), winner of the Pulitzer Prize.

Gary Snyder (1930–), essayist and poet, is the author of more than thirty-five books, including the Pulitzer Prize-winning *Turtle Island* (1974) and *The Gary Snyder Reader: Prose, Poetry, Translations, 1952–1998*. He is also the recipient of the Bollingen Prize and the Shelley Memorial Award.

Mark Strand (1934–2014), translator, essayist, U.S. Poet Laureate (1990), winner of the Bollingen Prize, and a MacArthur Fellow, began his career with *Sleeping with One Eye Open* (1964) and *Reasons for Moving* (1968). *Blizzard of One* (1998) won the Pulitzer Prize. His *Collected Poems* was published in 2014.

Wisława Szymborska (1923–2012) won the Nobel Prize in Literature in 1996. Her books in English include *View with a Grain of Sand: Selected Poems* (1995), *Poems, New and Collected, 1957–1997, Miracle Fair: Selected Poems* (2001), *Nonrequired Reading: Prose Pieces* (2002), and *Monologue of a Dog* (2005).

Dorothea Tanning (1910–2012), renowned painter, printmaker, sculptor, and set and costume designer, is the author of the collections *A Table of Content* (2004) and *Coming to That* (2011), the memoir *Between Lives: An Artist and Her World* (2001), and the novel *Chasm: A Weekend* (2004).

Alfred, Lord Tennyson (1809–1892), Poet Laureate of England (1850–92) and the most prominent poet in the Victorian era, wrote (among others) *Poems, Chiefly Lyrical* (1830), *In Memoriam* (1850), and *Idylls of the King* (1859). *The Poems of Tennyson*, edited by Christopher Ricks, was published in 1969.

Tomas Tranströmer (1931–2015) was awarded the Neustadt International Prize for Literature in 1990 and the Nobel Prize in Literature in 2011. His poetry has been translated into fifty languages. Recent books in English include *The Great Enigma: New Collected Poems*, translated by Robin Fulton (2006) and *Bright Scythe: Selected Poems*, translated by Patty Crane (2015).

Chase Twichell (1950–), a Guggenheim Fellow, is the author of *Perdido* (1991), *Dog Language* (2005), and *Horses Where the Answers Should Have Been: New and Selected Poems* (2010), winner of the Kingsley Tufts Award. She is coeditor, with Robin Behn, of *The Practice of Poetry* (1992).

Ellen Bryant Voigt (1943–), winner of a 2015 MacArthur Fellowship, served as Poet Laureate of Vermont from 1999 to 2003. Her books include *Kyrie* (1995), *Shadow of Heaven* (2002), *Messenger: New and Selected Poems, 1976–2006*, *Headwaters* (2013), and the essay collection *The Flexible Lyric* (1999).

Derek Walcott (1930–2017) received the Queen's Medal for Poetry in 1988 and the Nobel Prize in Literature in 1992. His books include *Omeros* (1990), *The Bounty* (1997), *Tiepolo's Hound* (2000), *Selected Poems* (2007), and *White Egrets* (2010). His play *Dream on Monkey Mountain* won an Obie Award in 1971.

Margaret Walker (1915–1998) wrote *For My People*, winner of the Yale Series of Younger Poets Prize in 1942, the novel *Jubilee* (1965), collections including *Prophets for a New Day* (1970), *October Journey* (1973), and *This Is My Century* (1989) as well as *On Being Female, Black, and Free: Essays, 1932–1992*.

Walt Whitman (1819–1892) published his masterpiece *Leaves of Grass* himself in 1855, bringing together within it his major poems "I Sing the Body Electric," "The Sleepers," and "Song of Myself." *Drum Taps* was published in 1865 and his final volume of poems and prose, *Good-Bye, My Fancy*, in 1891.

Richard Wilbur (1921–), U.S. Poet Laureate in 1987, is the author of *The Beautiful Changes and Other Poems* (1947), *Things of This World: Poems* (1956), awarded the Pulitzer Prize and the National Book Award, and *Collected Poems, 1943–2004*. He has been awarded the Frost Medal, the Wallace Stevens Award, and, in 1971, the Bollingen Prize for his translation of Molière's *Tartuffe*.

William Carlos Williams (1883–1963) is the author of the classics *Spring and All* (1923), *In the American Grain* (1925), *Collected Poems, 1921–1931*, with a preface by Wallace Stevens, *Paterson*, Books 1–5 (1946–58), *Selected Poems* (1949), and *Pictures from Brueghel*, awarded the Pulitzer Prize in 1962.

Elinor Wylie (1885–1928), a novelist as well as a poet, is the author of the collections *Nets to Catch the Wind* (1921), *Black Armour* (1923), *Trivial Breath* (1928), *Angels and Earthly Creatures* (1929), *Birthday Sonnet* (1929), and *Last Poems of Elinor Wylie*, with a foreword by William Rose Benét (1943).

Jeffrey Yang (1974–), author of *An Aquarium* (2008), winner of the PEN/Joyce Osterweil Award, and *Vanishing-Line* (2011), editor of *Birds, Beasts, and Seas: Nature Poems* (2011) and *Times of Grief: Mourning Poems* (2013), translated Liu Xiaobo's *June Fourth Elegies: Poems* (2012) and Bei Dao's autobiography *City Gate, Open Up* (2017).

W. B. Yeats (1865–1939), one of the greatest of twentieth-century poets, also wrote *The Countess Kathleen* (1899) and many other plays. His books include *The Wind Among the Reeds* (1899), *The Celtic Twilight* (1902), *Responsibilities* (1914), and *The Collected Poems* (1933). He was awarded the Nobel Prize in Literature in 1923.

Kevin Young (1970–) has written ten books of poems, including the trilogy *To Repel Ghosts* (2001), *Jelly Roll: A Blues* (2003), and *Black Maria* (2005). *Most Way Home* (1995) was chosen by Lucille Clifton for the National Poetry Series. *Book of Hours* (2015) won the Lenore Marshall Poetry Prize.

Adam Zagajewski (1945–), poet and essayist, is the author of *Mysticism for Beginners* (1997), *Without End: New and Selected Poems* (2002), *Unseen Hand: Poems* (2009), and *Slight Exaggeration*, all translated by Clare Cavanagh. In 2016, he received a Lifetime Recognition Award from the Griffin Trust for Excellence in Poetry.

Acknowledgments

For all of their foundational work in bringing this program into being, great thanks are exuberantly offered to Molly Peacock, Elise Paschen, William Louis-Dreyfus, Ellen Rachlin, and Howard Rothman of the Poetry Society of America. Past members of the PSA's staff who served as coordinators of the program include Timothy Donnelly, Matthew Rohrer, Andrew Zawacki, Justine Post, and Anita Naegle. Current PSA staff members who serve as devoted shepherds of the program include Laurin Macios, Programs Director of the PSA, Madeline Weinfield, Development Director, and Brett Fletcher Lauer, Deputy Director, whom I would also like to thank for his work on this book.

The New York City program was launched in 1992 with the help and enthusiasm of Alan F. Kiepper, President of MTA New York City Transit from 1990 to 1996. Thanks are also due to the NYC Transit President at the time, Lawrence G. Reuter, and to Thomas J. Savage.

This program has flourished with the support of Barnes & Noble, Inc., the Bydale Foundation, the Robert Sterling Clark Foundation, the Gladys Krieble Delmas Foundation, the Ford Foundation, the Lyric Foundation for Traditional Poetry, the Manhattan Delegation to the New York City

Council, the National Endowment for the Arts, the New York City Department of Cultural Affairs and Kate Levin in particular, the New York State Council on the Arts and Kathleen Masterson in particular, the Viburnum Foundation, and the Lila Wallace-Reader's Digest Fund. We remain supremely grateful to the agencies and foundations who are part of our history as well as those who provide ongoing support.

In 2012, the program was transformed by the creative energies of the current team at MTA Arts & Design, led by Sandra Bloodworth, Director, and Amy Hausmann, Deputy Director. Theresa O'Loughlin, MTA Chief of Creative Services, was key to the inspired new design of the posters. Donna Evans, Chief of Staff at the Metropolitan Transportation Authority, Thomas Prendergast, former Chairman and CEO, and current interim Executive Director Veronique Hakim provided continuous enthusiasm and support, which remains central to the success of this hugely popular and appreciated program.

We are deeply thankful to the leadership and staff of MTA New York City Transit for their contributions: Paul Fleuranges, Vice President, MTA New York City Transit Corporate Communications; Connie DePalma, Assistant Vice President, MTA New York City Transit Corporate Communications; and the Marketing team, including Robert Keenan, Gene Ribeiro, Neil Neches, and George Watson.

The friendship and happy working relationship between the staff of the Poetry Society and that of MTA Arts & Design is furthered by the contributions of Lydia Bradshaw, Lester Burg, Yaling Chen, Bridget Donlon, Tara Foster, Cheryl Hageman, Tamar Steinberger, and Rob Wilson.

Moments arise in significant undertakings and projects when "all hands on deck" is the only path forward. The dedication of esteemed members of the Poetry Society of America's Board of Governors and New York Advisory Committee has been crucial at such points. We salute PSA board presidents Ruth Kaplan (2008–16) and Kimiko Hahn (2016–) and give thanks for the special efforts of Catherine Woodard, Vice President of the PSA, Helen Klein Ross, Melissa Salten, Laura Baudo Sillerman, and Susan Soriano.

We wish to express our profound gratitude to the poets whose work has appeared in the program and buoyed up so many riders over this twenty-five-year period, and deep thanks to Jill Bialosky, Maria Rogers, Becca Kaplan, Jo Anne Metsch, and Drew Elizabeth Weitman at W. W. Norton for their contributions to this beautiful book. May *Poetry in Motion* flourish forevermore!

ALICE QUINN
Executive Director
Poetry Society of America

About the Editor

Alice Quinn is executive director of the Poetry Society of America. She was poetry editor at *The New Yorker* from 1987 to 2007 and at Alfred A. Knopf from 1976 to 1986. She is the editor of *Edgar Allan Poe & The Juke-Box: Uncollected Poems, Drafts, and Fragments by Elizabeth Bishop* as well as a forthcoming book of Bishop's journals.

Permissions

Art Credits

Index

Note: page numbers in *italics* refer to art.